FEARLESS NOW & NAMELESS

ALSO BY JON DAVIS

BOOKS

Above the Bejeweled City
An Amiable Reception for the Acrobat
Improbable Creatures
Heteronymy: An Anthology
Preliminary Report
Scrimmage of Appetite
Dangerous Amusements

CHAPBOOKS

Choose Your Own America
Loving Horses
Thelonious Sphere
Local Color
The Hawk. The Road. The Sunlight After Clouds.
West of New England

TRANSLATIONS

Dayplaces, by Naseer Hassan

FEARLESS NOW & NAMELESS

JON DAVIS

GRID BOOKS

GRID BOOKS
Boston, Massachusetts
grid-books.org

Cover painting: "The Burial," by Grant Hayunga.

Book design by Katrina Noble.

ISBN 978-1-946830-31-9
LCCN 2024951489

to "all the living and the dead"

CONTENTS

"It is the philosopher's search

For an interior made exterior
And the poet's search for the same exterior made
Interior."

— WALLACE STEVENS,
"AN ORDINARY EVENING IN NEW HAVEN"

"Even in Kyoto—
hearing the cuckoo's cry—
I long for Kyoto."

— MATSUO BASHŌ,
TRANSLATED BY ROBERT HASS

"The songs have changed; the unspeakable
has entered them."

— LOUISE GLÜCK

IN GIOIELLA

I was so new
I didn't know
what to attend—
the bells of sheep
or the huddle of them
flooding the wash,
the two bee-eaters
flashing coppery
on the slack wires
or the hoopoe
scuffling in the culvert.
I parked the rental
briefly at the dead end,
vicolo cieco, rather,
while the hoopoe lifted
its feathered crown
above the tall grasses,
a tourist himself,
having drifted in
years ago on a wind
much like the one
that swept *me* here.
If the wind had a name
it eluded me, as did
most things that week
among shepherds
and artists until
the untranslatable

dusk drew the light
out of the valley
leaving only the occasional
clatter of a sheep bell,
a breeze jostling
the night branches
of the cherry tree
thickening even
now with cherries.

AT CILL RIALAIG

If experience is what gives the world its shape,
the fundament and glyph, the harkening ear
of everything, then the frogs chorusing in the bog
are the heterodox archangels of County Kerry.
Or so I thought. I was walking alone from Cill Rialaig
to Ballenskelligs, joyful somehow in the cold rain.
The fields were green and calm, the stone walls
rain-slick and bright with lichen. The roadside
sheep were dripping, and the red-slashed ewe
had just given birth to a trembling lamb,
unbeautiful and bleating, the umbilical still dangling
from its mud-sopped belly. Torn, it seemed,
from my own imagination, my own body, torn
from the fundament. The rain pattered my hood,
and out in the Atlantic, sunlight shuddered
across the fog-bound Skelligs, Little Skellig
and Skellig Michael, whose gray stone flank
monks once climbed daily to worship
in the unremarkable air, while the lambs,
in the grief of it, in their separate flesh, took
their first frail steps, surprised, no doubt,
to be separate, to be alone and shivering
among clouds thick as wool, pelting rain,
the frog choir's annunciation and groan.

WALLACE STEVENS IN THE BLACKFOOT RIVER VALLEY

One would want snow even as the autumnal turns
Saturnalian. One would want the knuckled limbs
made stark by sunrise. When morning's heat
leavens the wasps, they'll scrawl nonce forms
across the window's bright page while the poet
leans over a sheaf between woodpile and flame.
In this romance, he craves a language to haunt
the ephemeral. Were he to lament, the sash
would burst into flame. Were he to celebrate, the moon
would lift above the cottonwoods abetting the creek,
the lone coyote would lance through high grass,
and the grizzly would sway, golden in that dawn.
The actual carries an exhausted charm mitigated
only by the imagination's refusal. What the poet sees
is a measure of his pain. What he hopes to see, a measure
of his mortality. When he finally writes, there is no fire,
no grizzly, no cottonwood, no coyote. He bears the cross
of the imagination over the hills of the actual.

KETTLING

> "Kettling apparently serves as a form of avian communication—
> an announcement of imminent departure—as well as a way of
> gaining altitude and conserving strength."
>
> – *Wikipedia*

Driving in October, once, I rounded
to a road-killed deer in sunlight, crows
and ravens, vultures leaping, squalling
above the bloody gorge of the doe's chest.
Buff-colored doe, black carrion birds,
all buoyant, sheened and battered
by brittle sunlight. Beyond was blue sky,
miles of grasses, an emptiness, leaning.
And in that emptiness, I remembered
my ten-year-old self stalking a crow-sized
woodpecker, the red-and-white flash of crest,
quick flight from pignut to pine, black wings
snapping shut, its bill like an axe
in the soft wood, chips flying,
the yellow gash opening, the *kuk-kuk-kuk*
and launch again, as I followed, feeling
a strange terror lacing that beauty. A terror
I felt again near the pine-lined creek
where turtles swam, wobbling the bottom,
dim stars on their backs, where I climbed
a hemlock and, twenty feet up,

a white-footed mouse, ephemeral
as the soul itself, skittered across
the feathery branches beside me. There,
I found the nest of the great horned owl.
Imperious, it tracked me while my heart
thudded my thin chest. Winter grouse
blasted from thickets. A great blue heron
battled a goose near dusk, a bluster
of wings, of claws and bills, of honking
and croaking. Prehistoric, they seemed,
in their frantic fall, until the heron flapped
its dusky wings and lifted itself backward
towards its nest in the shoreline pine.
For years, I wandered among log-rot
and leaf-mulch, toads and salamanders,
warblers fluttering and flicking through
brushpiles, the mist-dazzled deer stupefied
in the meadow, the squat woodcock,
meandering like a rodent, probing
the hummocks with his outsized bill,
looking perpetually surprised by everything.
Until, one dusk, he fluttered hundreds of feet
straight up on stubby wings to hover
a moment, buzzing and chirping,
before letting himself drop
earthward, catching himself just
in time to touch the ground lightly,
tuck his wings and strut. Meanwhile,
the vultures gathered and drifted, circling,
letting the heat from the valley lift them.

Kettling, they boiled higher, needing
height to achieve a vista, a vantage from which
to launch their long, rocking flights, wingtip
to wingtip, a hundred black crosses whirling.

THE RADICALS

They want to save my uncle from
ten hours a day, six days a week
of brick and trowel, trowel and mortar,
stone and hammer and stucco and block.
Want to save him from the cold
morning drive up the shore,
from fire barrel in the sand, from
choke and pull, from the mixer
rattling the calm, trowels knocking
mortar trays, leads built, line pulled,
the pure pace of running the courses.
From trowel's slice, from scoop
and butter, block up, swing and set,
from quick tap, scrape, begin again.
From calls for more blocks and mud,
the sun arcing over the long day,
Waylon crooning out the boom box,
flurries, light rain or sudden storm.
Want to save him from coffee shop
and roadside lunch, ham and egg
on a roll with ketchup, coffee
light and sweet. From banter and tease,
from hand-cut fries, double-burger,
iced tea. From Sal's big laugh.
From Carmen falling through a hole
in the deck, laughing in the sand below,
from Phil dropping his MG into gear
to race home, rear axle lifted

onto blocks, the wheels spinning
uselessly in air, from the college kid's
big words—*inundated, excoriated.*
From my uncle shouting, "Jonny,
we've got a plethora of mud here,
but a dearth of bricks." They want
to save my uncle from beers after work,
from David lugging two hundred pounds
of used bricks up a twenty-foot ladder,
from the flinty smell of stones
clacking stones in the truck bed,
from standing back at day's end
to appraise the stones in their new
settings—*that combination right there,*
rubble bond, smooth joints,
headlights snapped on to see it all
one last time before it's home to a beer
and a fire and the Yankees or Giants,
pasta with clam sauce and talk
and family and sleeping to wake
and dress in the dark to do it again.

ASTERISK AS ORNAMENT

Indicating neither *grave* nor *allegro*
and sounding, on the inner ear,
like a madrigal of zithers. A madrigal,
by which I mean a pale origin, a stasis

among the statuary, a blankness given
shape, a diminutive star. O, Aristarchus
of Samothrace, when you leaned
through candlelight, scattering stars

upon the text, you marked each absence
or untranslatable clause, each star-
crossed transit from crucible to crux,
as if absence were itself a passage.

AGAINST DELIVERANCE

My mother believed in nothing and to nothing was delivered.
        While firebirds circled the chimney.
While I drove from exit to exit, eastern Pennsylvania and nowhere to sleep.
        To sell a handful of books to the citizens of Nashville, I'd driven.
To see Rancid and my nephew and return.
        Driving was battering lights, darkness and fear.
Driving was twenty feet of road and music: "Lord, I'm going uptown."
        I'd been to Nashville and was returning.
When the call came, I could not answer.
        The last time I'd visited she said she'd read the online stories.
The last time I'd visited she said she now knew what I'd tried to tell her.
        I thought of him standing beside the bed, this "friend of the family."
But he never touched my boys, she'd said, digging into the *my*.
        My mother believed in nothing and to nothing was delivered.
While I drove through Pennsylvania near midnight without a place to sleep.
        The message said *She's passed.*
While firebirds circled the chimney.
        Gone as she wanted to be gone.
Despite everything or because of it.
        Four sons dead and yet she'd continued.
When I finally slept it was a dreamless sleep.
        Fine then, I thought, waking to a ceiling washed by parking lot lights.
Just go.

SARDONICA

My life has been a series of explosions—
first of water, then color, then a trauma
of words, a slithering trove of vowels,
a jackhammering in the consonant mine.

Therefore, have I been waiting for you
to see me, to coax me onto the bright page.
So tired am I of the lathered suits and lights,
the promenade of pundits who dream me

into their songs of blood and bombs. I
whose pixilated heart throbs in a caul
of kerosene. But who also trembles
like a needle riding black vinyl, relaying

the quavering nuance of every voice,
the voices of yearning and of the end
of yearning. There is powder in me
and fire, it's true, but each veil you lift

reveals yet another veil. Until you raise
the final veil and gaze upon this body
of light and wind, this emptiness
at the center of everything, this emptiness

whirling and stomping, lifting its skirts,
wild for wanting but also somber,
by which I mean shadowed. By which I mean
asleep and dreaming of gunshots,

I who was born for violence and cleave to it,
craving that shock which is elixir,
which shivers my body, though I long to be
an orchard at dawn, light rain, a few frail birds.

SPONTANEOUS KNOTTING OF AN AGITATED STRING

It starts with knotting and a knotting ends it.
All things flaxen in late autumn, when the storehouse
leans into winter's fictions. The tractor ascends

to ornament, lime green and livid yellow
beside the well-house, somnolent under a caul
of wind-drift chaff. It starts with knotting

and a knotting ends it. In winter when the ground
gives of neither fruit nor seed, the larks least larkish
under leafless elms. The leafless elms that lean and sway,

that vein a riven hillside, provoking an august twitter—
from the barrow ditch, a sudden burst of larks.
It starts with knotting and a knotting ends it.

IN ROOMS, IN LANGUAGE

And then it is a quiet afternoon.
My young mother, having left my father's ghost,

his unquenchable thirst and shell-shocked rants,
is dusting in another high-ceilinged room

dragging the vacuum and broom while I lay
alone with magazines and journals,

thin pamphlets from the New York Botanical Society,
the lawns, the shrubs and trees, a world

not unlike the gardens outside this house
my mother cleans so we can eat. The tall windows,

the antiques and patterned rugs. I must have longed
to be wealthy then in that empty house

turning from the botanical gardens
to the Zoological Society newsletter. If I understood

anything, I understood there was another world
not so much of leisure but of time. Time to attend

the lives of plants and animals, paintings in slick magazines,
essays cast in serious-looking journals

I ran my finger along, sounding out words I'd never seen before.
A life, that is, of the mind, which was, even at seven years old,

my only reliable world. A world where I could drop the curtain
on the careless days of event and brutality,

of brothers huddled in a bathtub
while our uncle leaned cautiously to poke the barrel

of the shotgun through the curtain-break,
the patrol cars idling quietly on the dirt road out front,

their lights flashing. The officers must have been
gathered near the cars, their service revolvers drawn,

waiting for our father. There were no
announcements, no calls to come out,

to surrender. Eventually, we were allowed to climb out
of the bathtub and walk into the bright light of the kitchen.

Where the adults ignored us, holding each other
one by one, then letting each other go. We were alive

then and safe. And the reliable night was already beginning
to assemble itself outside the window. All this before I knew

of cellos or knew the comforting song from the low branches
of the neighbor's hemlock was a wood thrush

or knew the fluted poems of Wallace Stevens
that awaited me in the paperback anthology

on the low shelves my great uncle Phil had built one weekend
and painted white; the same great uncle

who got my mother the job cleaning the house
where he repaired screens and painted trim. The house

where I learned, while the vacuum cleaner howled
in the distance and a slash of afternoon sun fell

across polished wood, and everything was ordered
and calm, that another life was possible,

though it seemed so distant that I could only hold it
inside, like the bright mints I discovered

in a ceramic dish that I tucked into my pocket
for later, or the magazines my mother said

I could take home and that I pored over,
but that offered me nothing, really,

that I could explain, just as the moon, calm and bright
over the willow, gone now these sixty-four years,

could offer me nothing, and so I took it all
and made of it a life in words.

A FEW QUESTIONS FOR M.

Will you be in town for the gala?
Bring a dish to the potluck? A sprig
of parsley? I love the word *sprig*, part *pig*
and part *sprite,* part *spring* and part *twig,*
as useless as parsley, as *garnish*—
part *radish,* part *garish,* part *garnet* and *gala.*
Will you coffee? Drink if you drink?
Sandwich if you sandwich? And let's
not get started on *drink,* kin to *brink*
and *drip,* to *blink* and *bring.* My memory
fails. I cannot, most days, recall the name
Suzanne Vega. That folkish song
remixed to a dance tune?
If one can reckon that arms-raised
sauntering *dancing*. But we've called
many things dancing. Even wars
were choreographed
until machines got involved.
Five days, I'll marinate in P-Town,
ducking the people who hope
to see me. Most are disturbed
by the errors I've made.
Like mistaking laughter for ardor
or ardor for a platonic coziness.
When the campaign ended, I discovered
someone breathing in my ear.
After that, the rains started,

Siberian elms sprouted everywhere,
and the waiter arrived with a plateful
of oysters. Imagine! And a champagne
mignonette! It must have been the anniversary
of some important convergence.
Once I watched a rainbow end in a field
filled with black-and-white cows.
Is it possible we could touch that mystery?
Or would it dissolve like that ghost
of a girl who wandered into my room
and came close to see what I was?
When I reached to see what *she* was,
she broke into a mist of color.
A *mist.* Part *missed* and part *massed,*
part *mast* and part *list*—an aid
to memory, a foundering ship.

INTENTION

Intention is a stuck gear, a starter that requires a hammer. Intention is a bottle of cheap Cava that won't open until it does, spraying the window and a shelf full of your favorite cookbooks. Intention is shaky on heels, too loud in cowboy boots. Intention snoozes under a sleep mask, keeps its ears plugged tight. Intention gets everything wrong—the pitch of the roof, the depth of the channel, the distance down the left field line. Intention is an ark for one of each species. A tunnel that turns out to be a cave. Intention meant to marry you but widowed you instead. Intention swings at the low outside slider every time. Intention won't wear its helmet, its elbow and knee pads. Intention tries to hit that impossible high note and squeals instead. Intention is writing its dissertation on *The Concept of Economic Fatalism in the Lesser Writings of F. Scott Fitzgerald.* Intention knows nothing, is cocksure about everything. Intention is a watering can meeting a Galapagos tortoise on the floor of an automobile showroom. Intention won't ever sit still. It bursts into meetings with a list of demands. Intention is a poisonous snake that you recognize too late. It's a long slow ride to the wrong hospital.

THE KETTLEFISH

The kettlefish, adrift, will mold its flesh
    to any circumstance. The tiger shark bumps it;
it becomes a jellyfish. Another jellyfish sweeps
    its cnidocytes across it and it becomes a thin,
impervious blade. But vulnerability, we are
    reminded, is required for creaturedom.
By which I mean, one must be eaten to be useful.
    One must be one thing, reliably, to be counted.
And so there is no kettlefish, though it,
    nonetheless, carries within it
a cataclysm of stillness, an absolute zero
    of silence, an essential crux
where becoming collapses into being.
    Because the flag of the imaginary
is pure red—except when it is black or green.
    It is purity that marks it most, its
canticle and peripatetic drift, a flag
    of vatic mist blown now across the wave crests.

UPDATE FROM THE CHAMBER OF COMMERCE

for John Gallaher

Now that the smoke has cleared,
we can see the menus and they are
surprisingly coherent—various meats
and sausages, multiple slathering
options. And the children who
survived the recent famine are
unexpectedly cheerful, waiting
in the garden with their mouths
open, hoping for just a few drops
of rain from the lone cloud
drifting now over the plaza.
And the plaza itself is crowded
with masked visitors—bearded
mountain men lumbering
through town for the annual festival
of roughhousing and horseplay,
wan *turistas* plying the alleyways
and craft emporiums, droll hipsters
looking for a hangry fix. Nights,
they remote their mechanical gates
shut, hoist their salt-bedazzled margaritas,
and toast the smoke-infused sunsets.
Still, officials are reluctant to declare
an all clear. The rabblerousers

who pulled down the monument
to our illustrious, though admittedly
murderous, founders remain at large.
And armed squatters from the South
have commandeered the Roundhouse.
But the views afforded the fortitudinous,
limited as they are by the "Closed
Trailhead" signs, remain impressive,
even as the crumbling adobe
in the city below casts
an incontrovertible pall
over the entire project. The mayor
asks only that visitors *not*
encourage the locals, who
are forbidden from galloping
within the city limits, despite
the clear popularity of the activity.
Selfies that feature the *caballeros*
are subject to confiscation.
Please note that the brawny albino
on the Arabian stallion
has been the subject of extensive
legislation, though he has so far
eluded capture. While recent
library acquisitions include
The Apocalypse & After: A Handbook
to Survival, one should not
gauge one's prospects by the librarian's
purchase orders. Surely a vague
allusion to apocalypse should not

put a damper, so to speak, on the fire
of a tourist's passion. We welcome you
and encourage you to explore
the *Zona Verde*, which has been fenced
and patrolled for your shopping
and dining pleasure. Be assured
we expect a bountiful fungus season,
and a handful of well-inflated
rafts will, with the assistance
of our recently assembled
mule teams, clear the narrows
and sail into the stagnant open,
an emblem of sorts for the bright,
though haunted, future
scheduled to appear
soon at an undisclosed location.

WALLACE STEVENS AT THE CRAFT FAIR

She beholds the coruscating millpond
and thinks *wind in the copper beach, a glissando*
of gilded leaves. The summer theater's

facade has paled. Touch-me-nots crowd
the cinder lot. And the ghost of art
stalks the leaf-garlanded streets.

The village arranges itself around tempera
and pottery, goods fashioned
in basements, on patinaed porches.

What impulse lately regarded brought
hand to brush and brush to paper?
Or placed clay on bat and spun it

to compliance? Estranged from our lives
so long that anything shaped by eye and hand
entrances. So a homemade song begins

with plucked notes on a mandolin,
a reed-thin woman's thinner voice.
A sympathetic wind begins soughing

in the willow's green cascade. Among
cattails, a bullfrog *harrumphs*, a redwing trills.
Connecticut, September, there is a comfort

here, a muted joy, a minor of art's
bright hope—to wake eyes and ears,
to charm us astray a moment

from computer screen and forced commute,
the too vivid *obbligato* of our days. She pulls
the curtains shut, if lace can shut,

and turns to the artless kettle, rattling now
and steaming, its hiss *un anuncio de nada.*
A bracing nihilism obscures the town gazebo.

THE FAMOUS POET

for Izzy

The family dog has escaped! Now even the famous poet must throw on his ratty sweatshirt and boots. Even the famous poet must find the keys that are probably in the pants he wore yesterday, that are probably in the washer. Even the famous poet must decide to walk the dark streets instead. He must trip over the skateboard in the middle of the walk. He must think, Who left a skateboard in the middle of the walk? Who made it dark out here? What sort of god engineers a big bang, a ball of gases, some carbon and oxygen, a spark of life, a one-celled organism, then two, some water, some plants, a swimming creature that crawls onto the mud flats, amphibians, reptiles, birds, mammals, primates, Australopithecus, neanderthal, homo sapiens, a stone age, an iron age, some dark ages, a renaissance, a skateboard, a punk in a beanie, a kick flip and a careless rush to dinner, an escaped dog, a brisk walk, a dark night, a poet? What sort of god lets the dog bolt between the screen door and the jamb and rush towards the street? And just when the famous poet had sat down to compose a sonnet! A sonnet about tennis and how tennis is so much like life—the serve, the follow-through, the return, the volley, even the net, yes, so much is about the net! The famous poet wanders through the neighborhood. He shines his famous flashlight into the shrubbery, behind the shrubbery, under the shrubbery. What sort of dog heads for the shrubbery? Surely there are loose dogs in the alleys? Surely there is some stinky trouble to get into? The poet remembers stinky trouble fondly. Surely there is a villanelle about stinky trouble awaiting him. But where is that dog? The famous poet never liked that dog. He secretly thought the dog would kill him while his wife and children slept. A quick nip to the jugular, and he'd have to forego the great poems of his later years. He flicks off the flashlight. Better, the famous poet thinks, that the dog wanders into the highway. The world needs the famous poet's later work. The ponderous poems of failure and death. The world doesn't need a rottweiler-chow mix who doesn't sit or lie down or roll over or come when he's called. They need a sestina about that dog! Yes, even the children would prefer a sestina, though they think they want to throw a frisbee and cuddle the dog, put ribbons in his fur at Easter and Christmas. But a sestina! The famous poet begins thinking of seven good words. Maybe *collar* because it can be used as verb or noun or even an adjective. Which reminds him of the Eurasian collared doves in the backyard and how all day they coo *kangaroo stew kangaroo stew* and the dog charges at them, and they flap ponderously just out of his reach. The worthless dog! The famous poet watches the night stars for a few minutes thinking about death and despair, then turns towards home. When he gets to the back door the dog is there, terrified, throwing his body at the screen door over and over, scratching, whimpering, and the poet thinks, *me too, buddy, me too,* and he throws himself at the screen and rips through to the other side and they tumble and skid together across the slippery floors looking for the humans—*where are the humans?*—shivering and whining and rushing down the halls, looking for the warm bodies that they find gathered by the television, and they throw themselves on them, their hearts hammering in their chests. They bury their faces in laps and hands and armpits and hair, howling and quivering, cooing and yelping, all of them, body to body to body in the flickering dark.

MISERICORDIA

Dawn and a light rain, first in a month,
chattering on the roof. And I think
of the house finch tangled in the fruit netting.
Dead now. And the fledgling thrasher
in the garter snake's grip, chirping while
the parents rattled—a call I'd never heard,
half warning, half mourning—and the snake
swallowing the bird whole, headfirst. It took
ten agonizing minutes, the bird's tail twitching,
the tender feet last to go. *All creatures brittle*
and hollow and brief. And here, in the poem,
I want to resist describing the raccoon family,
the young scrabbling from wisteria to weed bank,
from cover to cover, comical in their turn-taking,
their rapid footfalls, driven by a built-in fear,
a foreknowledge of the dangerous open.
To say they were slipping under the gate
and onto the road is to say what we already know—
divinity lives at the mercy of chance.
Always more of us than the world needs,
thus we continue, though each one of us
is meaningless—mouse crushed under the plywood,
bird dead in the hawk's talons, hawk hunched
under a mob of crows. Meanwhile, the revved
engines of want and anger, the needles and tinfoil
pipes behind the Allsup's dumpster—we wake
to our days and find our days intolerable.

We light up the screen, type in our passwords,
and the misery overwhelms us, while outside
the birds chitter and chirp. Poor birds,
each day like the previous one, filled
with food gathering and squabbles. Filled
with pursuit, quick mating, nest building.
With egg setting and turning and feeding
the chicks that will replace them. *Pecking order,*
we say, as if we were speaking of birds.

AN OPEN LETTER FROM MY POEMS

We have put off writing this letter, preferring instead to lurk and wait, hoping that you would discover us lying in the weeds beside the public thoroughfares and watersheds, here among the Joe Pye weed and thistle, among the discarded bills, the squashed masks and ejected beverages. But here we are, many years later, and nothing—not a word, not a slight quickening of the pulse, not even a quick nod of notice and dismissal. We have lived among you like dormice in a bell tower, like stale cheese that has fallen behind the crisper, or, as we like to sometimes think, in our better moments just before we nod off, like a treasured Bentley under a tarp. We are willing to accept our part of the blame. Clearly, we have been less assertive than we might have been, less, how shall we say this? confident? insistent? We have often been accused of being *jejune*, though we would insist our apparent naivete is a defense mechanism, guarding our deeper selves from the despair that would accrue from acknowledging our near-total absence from the world. We don't wish to flog this lifeless macaroon, nor annotate our crepuscular gravitas, but instead wish to suggest, gently, but with a conviction we have rarely been able to muster, that we, too, deserve, here in the concordance of our days, a seat at the table, with the grown-ups, if necessary, the yawners and leaners toward sleep, the jabberers and slurpers of soup, the slatherers of briskets and dismemberers of fowl. Long have we waited here in the breeze-wake of your Priuses, patient among the lost keys and hubcaps, for just a quick perusal, a look-see, a sideways glance. We might have something to add to the conversation, an opinion or two on eternity or a note on existence itself, that muddle of straw and mud, that concoction of vowels and consonants, that stumble of yearning, that quince aperitif, that clod of marl, that leverage of malaprops. We wish only to confuse the issue with a kind of clarity that clarifies nothing, a drop of amber that contains a drop of amber that contains a drop of amber that contains a bee. Or the *word* for bee, which, when spoken, releases a hundred bees into the world, all of them different, none of them real, but all dipping now to tumble in the depths of these actual tulips, lit as if from within by the light of the word *crimson.*

ON PRAISE

It's hard not to want more,
but more requires that you
repeat something you had,
perhaps, wanted to move past—
a way of being or doing,
an extravagance you'd hoped
to dabble in. But it became
everything, this praiseworthy
endeavor. Disappointing, yes,
but it will do no good
to shed praise like a skin, to say
you never wanted it. There's no shame
in wanting it, though it can be
a hindrance, a candelabra
that throws flickering shadows
in all directions,
until you become lovely everywhere,
but dissolute, vague, enshadowed
by your own desire, unsure if
what you are hearing is praise
or kindness. And kindness
is a draught of trickling
springwater, when what
you wanted was the flood
of praise, the whitewater of it,
the seaward rush.

A NOTE ON THE POETRY

While it's true I can't reach
where the flowers are, other paths
lead straight to that place
where announcements originate—
the pledge and the naming
of the student of the week,
the fourth grader describing
the cheese we can expect
should we still be hungry,
the new rules on parking
and the storage of household
poisons. You think the flowers
are a metaphor for the soul,
but they are actual flowers,
the rare cornflower-blue ones
that grow only on the mysterious
Islets of Langerhans, where
bagpipe music shrills the air
and the townsfolk dance
like they're in a Breughel painting.
The poets are searching for
duende, but someone forgot
to tell them he's a goblin, a trickster,
who shows up after the show
to stack the chairs on the tables
and sweep up. That's why
in the morning, your poem
tastes like sawdust, and the tinnitus

kicks in, making everything
rattle like a swarm of cicadas.
Don't even ask. You can't
get there from here—the lava
will shred your feet, and the air
is thick with locusts. El duende
wears wooden shoes and plays
a squeezebox. Even if you'd written
that poem, you wouldn't hear it
over the clomp and scuttle of the real.

WALLACE STEVENS ON THE MOON

Poetry, too, is weightlessness given form.
To hurry here is to walk like a man underwater.
The horizon curves and curves, a concordance
of mounds and craters, a crepusculum
deferring presence. One could choose
to praise this cinereal light or, limpid with hope,
hominify these estrangements. Because
poetry is a formal agreement to depose the venue
of the actual and launch a cadre of claimants,
a clamor of words, an emboguement, a clutch
of gravitas and trivia, we can conjure here
in this airless void, even as our labored
breathing rushes in our pulse-battered ears,
a petulance of petunias, a scrabble of larks.

LETTER TO HUGO FROM SANTA FE

Sunrise here slaps my tender cheek.
One moment, I'm dreaming of hard rain,
my long dead younger brother, next,
wham! the room is battered by brazen light.

I want the trees to slumber on,
to dream in shade a while longer.
I want clouds to lug their cargo
of rain into the valleys. In fact, I'm full

of wants, but the callow sun reminds me
there is no hiding place, nothing
I can keep and hold. The cars
on Agua Fria grumble, the motorcycles

shriek—a pandemic of complaints!
A plethora of competing wants!
My neighbors want it fast and loud;
I want this hawk to perch where I can see

the intricate regalia of stripe and scallop,
tail feathers stiff, soft underwing, cold eye,
beak stropping now against the bones
of a finch. Dick, I've never forgotten how,

when the sunset smeared that tiny classroom
window red, you rose and dragged your failing
body just to look. We were halfway to a rousing
dismissal of a student poem, but first

you had to see the sunset. Spring semester,
1982. You'd be gone by late October.
The whole class followed you to see.
When you sat back down, you sighed once,

glanced at the page as if appraising
a plate of squirming earthworms,
then raised your moon-face to pronounce:
"This poem could win a prize."

And we all shuddered, suddenly ashamed.
The sunrise in Santa Fe is like that,
wanting to fill every arroyo with light,
touch every chair and table with its genius,

glint off every piece of chrome. Who could blame
that hawk for wanting just one moment, furtive,
in the juniper, to slide its bloody beak
like a scalpel down that poor house finch's back,

to dip and stir the gristle and the meat,
to spread its wings and shield it from our sight.
In shadow, Dick, the poet's one true friend.

ON THE SPIRITUAL NATURE OF BIRDS

Birds now. Chattering on the wires,
the branches. Not the lemon-
breasted birds. Not the fierce wingers.
Not the inflight maters. Just these—
Shitepoke. Thunderpumper. Awestruck-
by-the-Unseen. We grant them intelligence
they likely don't possess. Though the ladder
has been folded and stowed, they return.
Mud and straw in their beaks. Hovering
over the absent ladder. As if.
What leads to what? Where the ligatures?
Where the duration? Memory to memory.
This *embodiment of the world's soul*, we might say.
Bird chatter. Leaf swoon. Dawn light
glinting along a wire. Say *birds*.
Say *chatter*. Say *chatter* to capture.
Say *chatter* to embrace the chirp. The chitter.
The snatch of song. The prayer flag flutter.
Say *chatter* and mean the sun. Aspen leaves.
The wind twirling the branches in its fingers.
Don't say *birds*. You'll get pelicans. Crows.
When you want dull sparrow. Not want.
Have. Even the house finch. Red blossoming
like blood from a neck wound. Is dull.
Who would claim spirit inhabits
a thing so dull? Who would say. And see.
In the dull plod of sparrow and finch.

Humping in the eaves. Gathering straw and string.
Laying the griefstruck and delicate eggs.
Flicking from yard to nest. Wing tuck.
Twitch. Hovering above those weaving
hungers, their beaks opened like hands.
Hands of a supplicant. Praying to survive
under the cold yellow eye of the thrasher,
that callow grifter who, given the chance,
would lift the bruised and bulbous
hungers lolling in the straw and string.
And drop them to the hardpan earth.
Not even the thrasher. Not even the finch.
Know why. Is that what spirit is?
The featherless infant writhing on caliche?
The mystery? The unknowing?

VOW

I promise what they all promise,
those makers of promises—
to love, and, because it's not these days
politic to say *obey*, to offer,
instead, a modest agreement
to not refuse to take the refuse out
or deliver a cup of coffee
to the morning bed. I promise
to love you until all talk between us
turns to grunt and sigh and barter,
until one of us thrashes all night
slugging the senseless pillow
until dawn. For now, let us
agree which lights to leave lit,
who will water which plants, who
dust when avoiding dusting
becomes a hazard. And let us promise
Sundays, when we'll sleep till noon
and, later, each of us on our separate phones,
read snippets of the world's
catastrophes and complaints.
Then maybe croissants, some coffee,
the sunlight leaning on its elbows
at the windowsill, studying our expressions,
wondering how we survive each other,
while the soundtrack shifts from your song
to mine—cello to power-chord—and back,

then a song we both tolerate though neither
with any enthusiasm. All this I promise—
as vague a promise as can qualify
as promise, but a promise I'd make no other.
At least not now. At least not here.

AFTER THERAPY, I REIMAGINE OUR LIFE TOGETHER AS A SERIES OF MOVIE SCENES

To say disaster is another name for Man is
to generalize from the particular man I have become.
Meanwhile, these dishes are smashable, that door
slammable. Here, I want to stop and say, I long
for the time before I became the problem, the trouble
banging on the midnight door, wanting to get
back in, ready to claim, dear Jesus of the skewed paintings,
Muhammed of the crimped Mustang, Buddha
of an emptiness big as a billboard, that I am forever
changed, here in my bedazzled jumpsuit,
my vague hair in a man-bun, my eyeliner a wreck.
After the credits, the outtakes in which I fumble
every important line and you sneeze out your gin fizz,
there is that long silence before the lights come up
in stages, a stale metaphor for my psychological growth.
See, it's a spectrum, from *Lost Cause* to *Manimal*
to *Fortress Defended* to a dynamo of carefully chosen
"I" statements. Like these: What I hear you saying is x.
Is that correct? As we move from indie drama to rom-com.
From rom-com to a fable filmed in the Australian outback,
desert in all directions and yet we slog inexorably
toward the horizon beyond which we have imagined
a glorious beach, waves breaking green to white froth,
emblems of hope and renewal, though the soundtrack birds
are, ominously, Brazilian. And my newly inscribed
adulting is as ephemeral as words traced across your back,

the *I* ♥ *you,* that, in the opening scene, made you turn
and smile over your tanned shoulder, but now
suggests a cutaway to terns lancing the waves
full of hope though they come up fishless again and again.
Is that a fair assessment? Am I reading you correctly?
What I'm feeling from you right now is what the room
must feel at 3 am when the ice maker shudders
and clatters, spilling cubes into an empty tray.

SUMMER, EAST VILLAGE

Three times
I stood
by your door

holding the red
rose
in my teeth, waiting,

until you finally
buzzed me in.
Blue, that door,

brutalist blue
under an amber,
chemical sky.

The foghorns
exhaled
& collapsed &

two youngish men
took turns
slugging each other

while a gaunt
woman, terrified
& dressed

for dinner, too,
        leaned,
    shimmering,

against a dumpster
        that *Wicked E*
    had tagged

in red & white.
        We slept
    windows open

hoping that something
        lively outside
    would quicken our hearts

so deft were we
        in those days
    so empty & so torn—

AFTER READING WITTGENSTEIN

Everything we see could also be otherwise.

– Ludwig Wittgenstein

The stunned apostles of science, who reveal all things—
the star-backed turtles and venomous snakes, the earth
curving into darkness, the languid, the sallow,
the undreamed-of bitterness—lectured nonetheless

long into the night, leaning into the fire, words
like seeds broadcast on a wind-burnished plain,
while the silence leaned in, a susurration of absence,
of *gone*, of long anticipation and finally no event,

nothing one can point to, no proposition in the deep
and moonless night. Forlorn, we were, and hopeless
in the gravidity of our days, the fulsome days of fear,
the virus circulating invisibly in our homes,

in the public squares. The virus had come for us,
was exploiting our strident politics, our
pronouncements and apologies, our quick-witted
comebacks and sorties. O, languid and somnolent ones,

O, wincers and leaners in the gruel of body and breath,
was there nowhere to hide, no canon of certainty,

no breath unbreathed, no uncontaminated surface?
We rose then, as if out of our sleeping bodies

and walked in the yawn and groan, the seep and flow,
citizens of a waning world first made of words,
then of digging and building, of thinking and building,
of arrogance and hubris. Like stevedores we were

among the tailings, our strength only to survive—
calculating, calculating, no end to our calculating.

WALLACE STEVENS AT TUOL SLENG

Beauty is unattached.

– Agnes Martin

A bird's plumage is made of plumes. Of this,
little is said, though much is made. The vexed
feather, they claim, invites the crosshatch.

A cliff is a crescendo of want. All the philosophers
agree. And further: *He fathers most who fathers least*
in the kingdom of clatter and cash. O, aesthetes in your

scholarly diminuendos, have you considered
the swarming of the mendicants? The one-legged,
half-blind men at Tuol Sleng, hands thrust

at the cowering tourists. Not lucre, they seek,
but the lucrative glance, the *here,* the moment's gift,
momentous in a momentousness, otherwise, of grifting.

Or consider a brighter morning—Boston, the sun
a cold white disc, snow glittering the railings, even
the beggars' eyes uplifted and haunted now by white.

A PENANCE OF CARING, A CRAMP OF NEEDFUL CRIES

My life has been a penance of caring,
a cramp of needful cries from another, darker room.

Friends blame it on a life I can't remember
living—the profligate one spent sunning

beside a vagary of waters, days spent following
memories and threads. The truth is I care

and don't know how not to. It's in my life not
in my writing; my biography's tangential to my craft.

I lived and yet my life slept sound beside my poems,
snoozing while my words were wide awake,

if width matters in such an undertaking.
They say machines will someday write our poems.

Well, good for them. They ought somehow
to know and live with failures such as these.

PREMEDITATIO MALORUM

The old people dealing cards at the picnic table in porchlight—
 a study in chatter and laughter and smoke, in yellow buglight and shadow—
are a comfort that grants us children this freedom, this courage
 to wander the edges of darkness, to leap at the moths that flutter

over our heads in the August heat, to part the grasses and search
 for the creaking katydids, to sit in the outhouse and stare
at the Hopalong Cassidy poster while spiders shake their webs
 in the ceiling corners. I try to name all the cousins daring the pathways

through the orchard—David, Linda, Kenny. I cannot remember them all.
 The flooded quarry is already half memory, half possibility. If I'd had the words
I might have said "this phenomenal dark," "this proffered bounty,"
 "this moment eternal." The orchard lifts its gnarled arms in moonlight.

August and the apples already rotting in the grass, all day swarmed
 by yellowjackets and black, wing-flicking wasps. A rising sweetness
in the humid air. House of yellow siding and thwack of screen door.
 House of lemonade and lace, of blue doors and crowded hallways.

Of bright bowl on a rickety table. Of lilacs and toads. Nighthawks
 meeping, whip-poor-wills whistling their names in the wild raspberries
and sumac. I am too young to imagine even the next moment.
 Caught between the evening's ruckus and the stars' scintillant quiet.

Caught in the drama of departure. While the uncles and aunts
 and cousins line up for their empty dishes and goodbyes,

I want to be everywhere and nowhere. Bluebirds
    in the orchard, box turtle in the pathway. A lather of tease

and counter-tease. A scrum of the unruly. I'm the one hiding
    in shadow, dodging the aunts' kisses and hugs. I'm the one
who crayoned his name on the outhouse wall. Soon I will be
    the one who must gather the younger cousins and herd them home.

Soon the bright sun will rummage through these lineages,
    these adenoidal boys, sorting them into the living and the dead.
A fistful of jacks and a ball. A pocketknife. A scattering of soldiers
    in their shale forts, patrolling the dirt roads, an anachronism of trucks

in a makeshift lot. I am thinking maybe time is the answer.
    Time that marks and scars us—the ruined berries, the poison ivy
reddening where it curls around the maples. Spume of spores
    above the puffballs. What is left for the imagination? Memory

is a knothole in a fence, a skewed view, a bend in the high-grass path,
    a black racer's waterslick tail going and gone. And later, sluggish pipefish
unscrolling in the sunlit shallows. Horseshoe crabs scuttling like tanks
    down the drainage channel from the treatment plant.

Another day and I'm in a city alley, *brrruming* a dumptruck
    beside the red-haired freckled boy I am told is David. Although
I don't know it yet, we'll soon be gone from this neighborhood.
    My father will stand alone in this same alley and turn red

with rage when he sees that his wife and boys have vanished.
    Time will have ruined everything. Or that is the illusion—time

as a succession of movements away from and toward, until suddenly
    I am in Santa Fe, New Mexico, wondering how anything,

anything at all could happen as it has, as it will. As it *must have*?
    But that is a religious question, and I
am six years old. God is the pollen in the air, the light
    breeze churning it, the sunlight dazzling it with presence.

AFTER THE DEATH OF POETRY

It was success that killed it. It had lived
peacefully in the small village of its making
for years. We'd see it occasionally, or pass
an open door in summer where someone
was standing at a podium and speaking
in that way we recognized, and we would nod
and continue with our day, assured
that it was surviving the way an endangered
tortoise survives, lumbering the endless desert
until it finds another tortoise, a small tuft
of grass. Or we'd see a line of thin books
in a bookstore, a stack of homely journals,
and think, good, they're still singing, this
oddly plain species, from the treetops and hills.
Their songs were not for everyone, knotted
and braided as they were, but we liked
that they were making and sharing them.
If we thought *bless their hearts*, it was more
to praise their devotions than to satirize them.
But then, things began to change. Their songs
got louder, simpler. They began appearing
on buses and trains, on screens, sounding
from street corners and bars and phones.
At times they ranted, at times they wept.
And an amazing thing happened: We started,
slowly at first, to understand
what they were saying. At last, we could stand
and cheer and not worry that we'd

missed the point. Yes, we thought,
your father was mean! Yes, the police
are brutal and, yes, racist! Yes, the yellow
butterflies bring us peace. They are emblems
of light and soulfulness and beauty.
And, oh, the patriarchy of it all! And
you loved your dog, but he died. And
that boyfriend truly was, as you say
so pointedly, a bastard! Now we can
grieve with you on this bus huffing
and swaying down Fifth. We can hear you,
my friends, as we wait for the DJ
to set up his turntables, for the woman
to tune her guitar. Soon, we understood,
everyone is a poet. Every utterance, once
spread across the page, a poem! Eventually,
we could no longer tell what was poetry
and what was talk. And that's the way
we wanted it. We realized that the poets
had been making us feel inadequate.
Even our unspoken contempt for them
had been driven by our feelings of failure—
failure to hear, to understand the complexity
of their writings. Now that poetry was dead,
really dead, we could finally enjoy it.
But then a strange thing happened. We started
missing it. The way you might miss a jungle
you'd never visited, a mountain you'd
only seen in photographs. We wandered
the streets hoping to lean into a gallery

and hear those cadences, those baffling
metaphors, see the audience members turn
to each other, sharing some secret,
some mysterious companionship
that made us envious. We missed
ignoring them, missed knowing they
were settling like a flock of robins
into an elm at dusk, chirping softly
as night filtered through the branches, sifting
finally into the bones of those dark, drowsing birds.

ABJECTION

after the paintings of Dirk DeBruycker

This is the beginning and the end, alpha and omega, the blotted-out place.
Here where the icons once paraded their sentiments.
Bleeding now because they cannot stop changing.
Bleeding now because they have been canceled.

If truth : beauty as *lamb : slaughter.*
Not Morocco. That, too, blotted out.
And Belgium. And Dirk DeBruycker.
And the author of these words.

Canceled.
Now we are figures in paper.
What we intended, gone.
Into filigree, tracery, into splatter and wash.

All the lines uncleated.
Now we mean *So much is lost.*
Now we mean *Can you hear us at all.*
Now we mean *What beautiful obliteration.*

Someone said *Help me climb over this barbed cancellation.*
Past these creatures gnawing at absence.
Someone said *Why such whimsy in the face of—*
Someone said *And all of it canceled.*

Canceled: The body, impaled and lifted above the marketplace.
Canceled: The body sprawled across the spikes.
Canceled: The fruits and vegetables uncrated, the lamb carcasses splayed.
All of it painted in another language.

The absence calling us to another language.
The absence which has become the darkness.
The darkness where the meanings once slept, tails curled, heads on their paws.
The bodies stacked and covered with canvas.

The babies who would not last the night without their mothers
(who had died of cholera) lain gently in the back of a truck to die.
Fifty infants. Smooth, babyfat hands closing on nothing.
Hungry, but not afraid of cancellation.

We were eating popcorn when we noticed that the truck bed—
in the repetition, in the contrast of rough cloth and smooth faces—
was achieving a kind of formal elegance.
Then a darkness canceled all of it.

A canvas flap pulled down for protection, for privacy.
An artist's brush.
There were six paintings on the wall.
I wanted to crawl into the one whose center was obliterated.

Into the O of orgasm.
Into the birth canal.
Into the crown of thorns.
Into the zero.

WITHOUT GODS

Miraculous machines, we are, honed
by history, shaped by each encounter
with sickness and pleasure, with tree
and bird and virus and song. "There is
grandeur in this view of life," Darwin wrote.
But we know almost nothing. With spools
of facts, with studies, with numbers.
We know almost nothing about destiny.
About beauty and joy. We carry on,
purblind wanderers on a barren heath.
How are we all not like The Shouter?
Who drags himself and his cart full
of possessions—a tumble of blankets,
garbage bags full of clothing, boxes
emptied of food but saved nonetheless—
who stops at each corner of Fifth Street
and shouts at nobody, or at somebody
he has invented, some father or brother,
some incendiary someone. It's always
a growl, a protest, a plea, a need. Only
once could I make out the words. "That
was mine! You took it! It was mine!"
Then: "I see you there! You can't hide!"
I had been leaning, looking through
the fence slats. I wanted to see him.
Did not want to be seen. But he
was not shouting at me. He was never

shouting at me. And so it went
that summer. My stepson and I
remodeling a house, poorly built
and badly rebuilt over successive
generations and owners—the floor
crooked and unsupported, plumbing
no longer ferrying the waste properly
to the sewer, asbestos tiles, mismatched
finishes on the walls, a fireplace
without a damper. Every new project
required us to go back to the beginning.
Back into the crawl space to jack
and level, prop and scab, while,
outside, the homeless dragged
themselves from shelter to handout.
And the neighbors posted their
weary complaints, built fences,
locked mailboxes, mounted
their security cams. Once, in the caves
of what we now call France, fifty-seven
thousand years ago, Neanderthals
gathered to rake soft clay
with their fingers, to say we were here,
we shouted, celebrated, complained,
we lived and died in darkness
and to that darkness we were wed.

JESS

Everything has always been endangered. You, me,
the maroon trillium that unfurls above the pine needles,
the lady slippers in the clearing, the moment
when the sun stuns the reservoir's dark surface,
and the white heron rises to flee the danger—
the two of us wandering down the shore
to the endangered island. All along the water's edge,
the endangered sundew plants wait for the ants
and midges the way we waited for something
or someone to whisper in our ears, saying this
is it, this is what you were looking for, some angel
of the ordinary, some friend, some lover, some
solid thing, some unendangered stillness
in the general swell of uncertainty—clouds
coupling and uncoupling, the waves the winds
groomed and sent shoreward, the squawk and leap
of the bullfrog, the lunge of the bass.
Danger and uncertainty everywhere and what
to do about it? Once we swam in this illegal water
while someone you knew tossed rocks at us. First,
golf-ball-sized rocks that we dove and dodged,
then bigger rocks that plunked around us, then
rocks as big as our heads, crashing beside you
while you treaded water closer and closer to shore.
He said nothing, nothing at all, while you
laughed hysterically and taunted him. I did not,
in that moment, know who you were. When he

finally got bored and left, you tried to call him back,
and now I see that you were already the person
who would flash a handful of pills and gulp
them all, then stare at your face in the hallway
mirror to see what you might become, or take
too many hits of acid and sit back in your father's
music room, in his lounger, like a man strapped
into the electric chair and let Jim Morrison's words
stir your muddled brain. You spent your last days
making paintings of doors and windows and ladders,
then leapt in front of a semi, headfirst on a rainy night.

GRACE'S SONNETS

1. DAUGHTER

And who are *you?* Nope. Don't have a daughter.
You call that my hand? It's hardly mine.
I'm sure you're lovely. Where's my water?
Now find someone to turn this into wine.
I remember things. Mostly songs.
I liked to swing and sing in summer wind.
The one about the *dogies* and *git along*.
They used to say your knee was *skinned.*
I would like to speak to the management.
That's the sort of thing I liked to say.
If you're my daughter, I'm the president.
Sure. *You* can leave, but *I'm* stuck here all day.
    All wavy in the willow wind that orangey bird.
    Was sometimes seen but almost never heard.

2. RAT-KILLER

Grace. What a name for a rat-killer, right?
Smacked it hard with a Louisville slugger.
Sat up in a kitchen chair, waited all night.
Whacked it at dawn, then had tea, one sugar.
Enough. It tires me to think and speak.
That television, though, is mostly noise.
And this room smells like rotten egg. It *reeks.*
Blue is mostly word. But red's a choice.
It's a simple ask. More air and light.

You should get a job where you stand and stare.
You're right. I don't trust windows at night.
I liked to dance, but not like Fred Astaire.
    Nature was mostly a disappointment to me.
    Not like the TV shows, a macaque in every tree.

3. M&M's

Frugiverous. Now there's a word to remember.
Someone died, left me in charge of everything.
The song says thirty days: *April, June, November.*
I look at my hand. All I see: a golden ring.
Is it still two o'clock? Seems it's always two.
I told George to kill those mockingbirds.
If you have those M&M's, I'll have a few.
They chatter all night. Can't make out a word.
Can you get Stuart to bring the car around?
Is that a song I hear? Some god down in it?
Was blind, was lost. But now I'm found.
Someone needs to get the shears and thin it.
    Bell-bottomed pants. Think *they'll* make a comeback?
    I was dull, my mama said. Dull as a thumbtack.

4. BOB BARKER

Bob Barker? Smarmy? For sure, but what a tan!
I remember reading every book on these shelves.
Had time for dogs, they say. Not much for humans.
It's shadows of the things, not things themselves.
I'll have that round bread, toasted, and with butter.
Do they still call them Alps, those mountains?
I loved mornings in Paris, evenings better.
It was the sixties. We romped naked in the fountains.

There was music then, *in the cafes at night.*
I saw Dylan when he stormed the Bitter End.
Ragged but we loved it. That guy could write.
When he went electric, I thought I'd lost a friend.
  If I listen really close, I hear time ticking.
  At the end, my husband answered every question *Chicken!*

5. TURN

There's a voice inside my head. It's not my own.
Shhhh. Can you hear it? Listen close.
It narrates my every move in a booming baritone.
These are my going-for-a-country-drive clothes.
My husband will be here soon, you'll see.
Shows up once a week. Recent death be damned.
Okay. Not so recent. Ten years seems like three.
Life is never so long or sweet as we demand.
We hiked in Cinque Terra, those grassy hills.
You'd think they'd turn the lights off while we sleep.
My memories are sharp. It's those blue pills.
The lights stay on, but then they cut the heat.
  You're waiting for the turn? Don't hold your breath.
  The only turn I know's this turn towards death.

HUNTER JUMPER

for Grayce

The announcements were random
and seemed unrelated to the cantering
and leaping, the girls in their helmets
and jodhpurs, their ponytails flapping
like the horses' actual tails, though
with less regulation. And the parents

scrabbling along the course with cameras,
their hearts dubstepping in their chests,
their camcorders shooting grass, shooting
juniper, shooting occasionally someone's
daughter aboard some mortgaged beast
with hooves the size of a young girl's head.

LEGACY

Who taught these women the flutter
And shriek, the panicked cry that crests
To stop the lean of furniture, shatter of vase,
To yank the child from the brink of flame?

Schooled by disaster, the everyday spill,
Taunt of wind blasting the treetops?
Or was this panic handed down,
A birthright more nerve than thought,

Winter's legacy, a trauma in the blood,
The tilt toward death that shows itself
When cold wind saws on the frail bones
Of a northern house? The men, too,

Shriek, but, being men, swallow it,
Let it plunge in the darkness
Of the body. They'll plumb it with drink
Or try to quell it, I should say,

While waves storm shiplap and stone,
Their hands conjuring things
That won't quite last the winter—
A fire, a stew, a song, a thin beam of light

That falls just short of the beast
Maraduing in the barnyard, its eyes bright
In the brittle darkness, stomping
The hay rick, upending the cart. It goes on,

Life does, cambered and cracked,
Untempered by the shrill weathers of our need.

THE WORLD'S PRAYER

We are the hand caught in the gears
that brings the machinery to a halt.
We are the arsenic in the world's
bloodstream, the plastic in its gut.
We are the moaning and the sigh.
But don't the finches
sound lovelier in our ears?
Won't they miss our steady attentions?
Will their songs be as lovely
without our judgment, their breasts
as red without our eye?
They'll still bicker and flutter
and weave their flimsy nests
while flowers in the meadow below
entice bees as they always have.
And the bees will succumb
to the wasps and the wasps die
by parasite or bird.
And, in this way,
a balance will be achieved.
Without us cheering for this
or that outcome. Without
us cheering for beauty and virtue,
for the defenseless and trembling.
O, Lord of flight and falling, too,
Lord of tooth and claw.

It was love that tore this down—
love and pity and fierce devotion.
It will be love that builds it back again.

A STRUCTURE FOR OUR GRIEF

Build it of plastic that lasts a million years but quickly comes unhinged and unglued and gets left at the curb to be lifted onto a truck by mechanical arms and taken to the landfill, where it gradually decays into flakes and chunks, some of which are eaten by gulls and terns, who fly off to the ocean and shit while they paddle the waves until a whale comes seining and swallows that plastic along with all the other plastic—the bottles and cheap sunglasses, the ghostly bags—and its digestive system clogs and fails and the whale, starving, begins thrashing and groaning, and the other whales gather and try to comfort it while it founders and dies and floats to the ocean's surface where birds and fish feed on its carcass and the waves eventually push it gently onto a beach where the sunbathers and swimmers find it, gathering around to look at the hole where the eye was, the half skeleton half flesh of the fluke, until they can't stand the stench and head back to their blankets and coolers and sunscreen, while the other whales drift in the distance, rising to blow and diving back to the depths to mourn, sounding their squeaks and clicks, deep hums and squeals that can be heard, scientists say, by other whales four thousand miles away.

BECAUSE I DID NOT KNOW HOW TO DIE

Because I did not know how to die,
        I continued
to live. And, in living, denied death
        with every glance,
with each rose savored as it
        curled and dried
and fell toward its own demise. How

simply the flower dies,
        petal and pistil and stamen, leaving behind
the immortal vine.
        Immortal because it lives one moment
longer than the flower,
        and, in that moment, all possibility,
all hope, survives.

I did not know how to die so I continued
        this wandering
among monuments and flowers, among words
        like *love* and *tomorrow*,
our kisses growing less and less frequent,
        though we held each other
in the wake of loss, held each other

in the sunlight
        of our emptying days. I did not know
how to die, so I walked
        out into the darkness where the branches

swayed and the moon
        appeared above the mountains, a still point
the earth rolled toward,

as we roll and disappear one by one, like stars
        in the ensuing dawn.
Are you there? Yes, but fading. Then gone,
        leaving only traces—
a train of glances and whispers,
        damp with dew,
disappearing over the threshold of the day.

IN MEMORY OF MYSELF

Soon enough, I'll be just a wayward thought,
a window-glance while you rinse the dishes:
clouds draping mountains, sun
slashing through, torching the valley's pale green.
Or maybe blue sky, bright sun—another day
like the last. I don't know what I mean to say
with all this talk of weather outside a window.
I, who loved weather, the way it went on regardless,
embracing even the steady drone of sunny days.

But I was mostly fear when I walked the planet,
mostly a child huddled inside a man's body, filled
with grief and worry. And always hungry. I remember
eating from the sugar bowl. Three years old.
The only food there was. And rage was blazoned
everywhere, until I began to breathe it in
and carry it inside me. I thought I could keep it
there, the way scientists once thought they could
safely fold uranium back in the fissured earth.

HYLOZOISM

In the soul fused to molybdenum, in the caliginous
lungs of the sulfur caves, the arc of the caryatids'
sleep. In the storm's lucid dreaming, its muttering

and pacing at the edge of town. The faint pulse
haunting the girder's wrist. The squalor of mica
and galena, tumbling from the griefstruck rift.

The trenchant boulder lecturing the rain. The dead
stump's afterlife among the flames. All of it imbued.
All of it afflicted. As we are. In the flutter and sway of time—

the past arriving from the stars; these earthly moments
drifting out through the atmospheres. My brother
just now dying again on *Mu Arae b*, fifty years

after the crash. The motorcycle's steel and plastic
will soon be heard moaning under canvas there,
on that tiny planet that circles its iron-hearted sun,

hardened by billions of years of witnessing, enflamed
by billions of years of helplessness—the car turning,
the motorcycle's steel and chrome first screaming,

then sobbing quietly in the roadside thicket,
where the young man's body lay, soon to be inert,
soon to be alive the way smoke is, the way stones are.

ON LANGUAGE

> "... for recently the wave of Lethe's waters, *seeping*,
> *lapped* my brother's *pale* foot."
>
> – Catullus

Words have will, have heads and tails, have wings
sometimes, and fly us far from where we thought we'd go.
What Catullus wrote still nests inside these vowels.

The anguished etymologies flip from earnest to ironic
to iconic in a decade. Already I'm far from my intentions.
I meant to say, I long for wings, for flight, where *flyht*

meets *vlucht*, where what I want to say succumbs to fear
or, on a lucky day (*luck,* from Middle Dutch, at first
meant fortune neither good nor bad, so death by fire

or sudden trove of gold were both called *luck*), my imagination
flies. *Bon chance* we say, to distinguish good from ill,
my last living brother, for example, easing through

the intersection—was blasted from this life. I excused myself
from the meeting and took my mother's call. She could not
say the words. My guess was one word only: "Wayne?"

The third brother to die that way. It seemed impossible,
but such is *luck. A man makes his luck,* some say. Don't
believe it. The light was green, the weather clear.

Morning birds were no doubt raucous in the trees.
The truck pulled slowly out. Someone ran the red.
The luck was bad. And here I am, flown so far

from my musing about words—*so filled with meaning*,
Derrida might say, *they mean both everything and nothing.*
This everything will not let go its grip on me.

WALLACE STEVENS ON *L'AVENUE DE LA MORT*

Pigeons squabble the balustrades,
unrequited in their jostle for position.
Below, the human fervor of regret
and revenance—lost wallet, eye

swole shut, the battered man
scrawled across the sidewalk. None
lament his ashen face, frostbitten hands.
He'll be a frieze of promises soon,

lost in his cauterizing brain
like every mortal. The unforgiving sun
will blast his concrete bed; rain
concatenate and bristle in the grass.

The grist of philosophy is the *fin*
of every *siecle.* Death resides
complacent in a scrim of words,
while men saw planks

and hammer coffins tight.
No ontology salves the martyred man.
When, for the first time, he sees stars,
the cluttered sky's a glyph for grandeur,

a malevolence shorn of grievance.

ON MISSION HILL

Desperate in the surge and cower
of his seventieth year, he scrambles
above the others. His wife, daughter,
son-in-law, granddaughter stare up,
as if they mean to call him back. If
there is a metaphor, he does not see it.
He pulls himself along a fallen log.
At hill's crest, a layer of tufa
has spread itself across the bedrock
like a skull cap—an explicable strangeness,
unlike the textured grief he is feeling—
like sweetgrass braiding in his mind.
He cannot tell what strands
when braided carry what sadness—
is it death of a brother twined
about a failed marriage? Faithlessness
wrapped with the daily terrors of lugging
childhood trauma like an unconfessed
sin to the communion rail? Forgiveness,
he understands, is no good. It says
keep going, keep going, like Lear
through the storm-shattered night.
One would need a wise fool
or an ultimatum to fix this.
When he was thirty he might
have thought he'd lose himself
with a lover, dinner and bed
and a sunny morning with eclairs

and glass cups of espresso, the small
spoon *tinking* the cup sides like
golden bells. But then came the long day
of chores—and delights which began to seem
like chores. Could it be, as Stevens wrote,
the people of paradise feel *some*
small minor of what we feel?
We are fulsome in the arbor, stunned
by light glinting off the thin river
tumbling over granite, pierced by a child
kicking and babbling in her grandmother's arms,
as if she would float off into the bright day,
a cherub kicking her way across the meadow.
Look at me, she will seem to say, aloft
in the beneficent sky. Such miracles
he imagined, then, appalled, hoped
to call them back. Because the truth is,
we are trained to the leash. The truth is,
he would begin running beneath
the chosen child kicking and giggling
her way over bluebells and asters and daisies,
because he would not know when
the spell would break, when the angels
holding her up would tire. Faith says,
whatever will be. Faith says, we must
let it happen, as we always have, our hands
light on the tiller, steering between rock spur
and whitewater. All of creation shrugs.
Fate? Happenstance? A curated
succession of events, but curated
by whom? The unanswerable knock;

the groaning sound the moon makes
pulling itself over the eastern edge;
the wave-song like a mother humming
a rolling lullaby. Seventy years, he thinks.
With luck another twenty. After that,
oblivion and crumbs. And every miracle
like this one—the tufa fitted over the basalt
like an eggshell—and *as brittle. Look!*
he wants to say, but everyone he wants to show
is hundreds of feet below him. He is a poet
so understands wanting to pour out
a truth that becomes, instead, a mere
pouring-out. He kneels and turns the tufa
in his hand. Such a common strangeness,
worth, probably, nothing. He chooses one
characteristic chunk and turns
to go down. Then tosses it, too. The sun
is everywhere, the sky a brilliant blue.
The aloneness that once cheered him,
that held him up if he leaned into it
or pitched him backward if he forgot,
seems less sufficient now. He doesn't know
why he invented the image
of his granddaughter pedaling herself
happily across the sky. Or why he needed
to climb alone to the top of Mission Hill.
He must have mistaken scale for heft.
He could see where he'd flung himself
over the first ridge. Hadn't he heard
his daughter call him back? He'd hurtled

upward anyway. Some clumsy need
he couldn't name, some drive
that drove him into drivenness. Suddenly,
he wanted to, before it was too late,
let go, finally, of ambition's pull,
and sit and listen to their stories,
the blasé vernacular of a day, a touch,
a wren instantly, for no reason, incarnate
above the woodpile, burbling brightly,
then as quickly gone, tucking itself
into the comforting tangle
of viburnum, trillium, Solomon's seal.

THE CABIN

After which, a listlessness
settles in, like ash from a fire
in the mountains, like dust
during a prolonged drought,
the way it spreads itself
equally on the table, the plate,
the fork, the ceramic cup,
the setting mysteriously gracing
the warped wooden table,
set at one end, as if awaiting
more settings, a gathering
of family, perhaps, or old friends.
Have I walked in on myself?
Twenty years hence, living alone
in a rotting cabin at forest's
edge, sleeping until noon
then stumbling onto the stoop
to throw bread to the magpies
I have named Little Death,
Shadow, Lucifer, Hexmaster,
Grump. Afternoons, I scuttle
the birds, then lean to the text
of the book I wrote long ago,
running a bent finger
across the words, speaking them
aloud slowly as if each one were
new, as if, somehow, I could
remember who I had been, restore

myself to an earlier way of being,
                                        though the magpies chatter
and creak in the willows
                                        all day and the black bears sway
as if to scare me inside. But I
                                        am fearless now and nameless.
Part light, part water, part wind,
                                        I have left a long
trail of words behind. Now,
                                        in the meadow
along the river, the wolves
                                        have picked up the scent.

THE GATHERING

for Bob and Brenda

Tipsy though we were, we parked the rental
on the breezy bluff. Gray stones and sheep,
a clatter of waves and wind, three poets
chattering about Shakespeare's sonnets.
Then a scuffle of feet on the stone path,
and Seamus, ten years gone, white shock of hair,
reading by the fire, charming the women
who crowded the bar. Celebrating, we were,
but no one knew quite what—
this passage through air, through rooms
and airports, the fragility of it, the brevity.
We did not know how isolated we'd been.
We'd come out from our homes surprised
to find ourselves unmasked, our bodies
blinged with light and song, the living
and the dead equally at home here.
Here on the Irish coast above the breakers.
There was far to fall and fast. Such was life:
A calling, a fatal falling, but the talk was good.
Books and whiskey, the breath to say
whatever kind or unkind thing—jest
or gesture, some grand theory of everything.
Mostly I recall how we leaned and spoke
like we meant it. And we did, though
we were ephemeral as the terns that scissored

the blustery sky above us, or more so,
there on that improbable bluff. Not even real,
just dream people in our white shirts, wild
somehow about the way words fit together
like fieldstone in a wall. The cobbled wall
that, someone said, would last another
thousand years. "A marvel," Seamus said.
"One of many." And a sadness palled us then.
For we were dying. Or already dead. When finally
someone thought to stir it, the fire ring was cold.

FLAMENCO RECITAL

for Maxine Rael Zayas

That she could give herself to it
so completely, that she was present
to the goodness of it, whatever it was.

That the sunlight kept shouting
yes, & the wind. That she
was laughing & clapping

& holding her friend's arm.
That we were witnessing it. That she
was alive in the trust of it,

the red & white of it, the twirl
& stomp of it, that we were all
in the twirl, the stomp,

the singing & shouting. That the sky,
whatever it was, was making itself
blue, the trees an impossible green,

that we had gathered for this
twirling & stomping & clapping.
That it would end

& go on forever, too. Whatever
we mean by *end.* Whatever we mean
by *forever*. The sun, the sky,

the twirling & laughing,
the night waiting
at the edge of the forest

with its satchel of stars, its pale moon.

OF LIGHT AND TIME

In the old photograph: four men and one woman.
Probably in their twenties, which is to say
five people deeply aware of their own mortality,
having recently discovered it, and probably
most interested in getting high and fucking—
or doing anything to forget about death.
Like taking the motorcycle—the black one
that dominates the foreground—onto the highway
and cranking the throttle until they've gone
beyond fear, into the realm of the nerves,
like their friend who lost control on Route 8
and dropped his Harley sideways, and held on
as it skidded beneath him at eighty miles an hour,
then seventy, sixty, sparking and scraping, until
it finally stopped, and he stood, himself a miracle
in the miraculous night, unharmed. And kicked
the bike into life again and wobbled it home.
I am sorry to report that he shot himself
in the head in his old bedroom in his parents' house
two weeks later. But he, for obvious reasons,
is not in the photo. In fact, the photo is so blurred
I cannot tell you exactly who is sitting on the stoop
or the stone wall or standing in the shadow of the porch.
Most are probably gone. The photo is fifty years old.
And death by motorcycle, death by car crash, death
by the slow decay of the tormented body all came
to take them one by one. Though the photograph

suggests music and protest, a festival, a meaningful
existence, it was only a style, a way of dressing,
a way of wearing one's hair, a frisbee, a hacky sack,
beachballs launched into the crowd and cheered.
Though let me tell you, when I was in the middle of it,
strumming the guitar I owned but could not really play
or climbing the Green Mountains to look down
at the valley, the Winooski River cutting through forests
and fields, or listening to late-night college radio,
the whispering DJs, it felt like we were on the cusp
of something. Of what, I could not—I cannot—say.
What I can say is that whatever bright hopes we had
turned dark after midnight, turned into biker gangs
and rifles, armor-piercing shells and stolen whiskey.
Some rage to live made us thieves and gamblers,
druggies and drinkers. And here is where the film
stalls, where the acetate flames out in the projector,
the screen blares white. Not quite alone, I survived
to tell the tale. But it is not a tale with a moral
or a meaning. It meanders like the Winooski.
It does not explain God's ways to man. It is a tale
that stalls and stops like a saddled horse cantering
a dirt road. In Vermont, say. She has thrown
her rider and cantered on anyway. And now,
finally, she has stopped beside a spring,
where the grass is tall and green, like a dream
of grass, the spring itself like a spring in a black-
and-white photograph blurred by light and time,
the sun glancing off what must have seemed
a delicacy, the cold pool that the horse leans to,

huffing and drinking, deep and long, lifting her head,
finally, to see that she is alone, free, and what
that might mean, ears twitching, trembling
and glancing, stomping now in the poisonous dusk.

CARNAL IN THE LAND OF BLOOD AND BEAUTY

for Grant Hayunga

To make of fur a furred thing. To make
of fur a doe who is surprised to be a doe
who walks upright in the blood and danger.
To make a wolf lunging over marbled snow,
a falcon among flowers, a hare
bemused by a raven's headstand.
To make not only the night branches,
but the quavering owl [not pictured].
One way is to make everything look
like everything else; the harder way
is to make everything look like itself
and more than itself. Golden,
the cloven field, and the live oaks
nostalgic in the winter of their intentions.
The pronghorn's gaze radiates a wary
equanimity amid the burgeoning. Meanwhile,
the somnambulist wanders the blue night,
crows rise on wings of black flame,
and the skies grow menacing, if by menace
we mean the trees' stark clarity against the bright
omen of cloud. *Omen*, we say, a sound
more lips than tongue—half *ominous*, half *amen*.

WHAT MEMORY IS FOR

My uncle has something to say, so
he begins a sentence. "That's the guy
right there, the one leaning on the nurse's
station, wearing his whatchacallits." But
when he tries to complete the sentence,
there's nothing there, so he says, "That's
the guy who does everything, and then
he goes down, down, down, and then
he has to turn it over, turn it over,
and then everything goes to the doctor."
Which is the kind of thing my uncle
kept saying yesterday in the rehab facility,
while, on the muted television, some
twelve-year-old from Taipei threw,
improbably, eighty-mile-per-hour fastball
after fastball, a phenomenon that
ordinarily would have intrigued my uncle,
but he was focused instead on staring
at the remote as if it were some exotic
artifact from a civilization he knew almost
nothing about. And, strictly speaking,
that was true. I must say here that I'd
intended to write about memory, about
about what it is for, what purpose
it serves in a meaningful universe.
How without it, everything is a threat.
We cannot find our way home, cannot
reliably go anywhere since going requires

having been and having been requires
a constant monitoring of our progress
through space and time. But maybe
that's too grandiose. My uncle,
delicately and carefully, and I think
maybe ruefully, too, picked thin hairs
off the sweatshirt the nurse had loaned him
from the lost and found. His rhythm
was like a brush on cymbals, a way
of keeping time in a manageable, for him,
arena. He dropped each hair to the floor,
then started looking for another. I began
to understand that he might decide
that life is too hard, that a life without
memory is a butterfly fluttering
over the impatiens, buffeted by breezes,
rerouting itself toward whatever flower
presents itself. Because even syntax
is not a promise, but an adventure,
a fluttering in brisk wind. And isn't that
what the holy people praised? Without desire
every moment is perfect. Serene.
Without time, we are, each of us, butterflies
in late August sun. But the other possibility,
that the butterfly's flight is protection,
the erratic, a defense. Which, if true,
means memory itself is a threat, makes us
cautious and predictable, until we stream
through life guided by habit, the foliage
a kind of invisible backdrop, the people
a throng of obstacles trying to freeze us

in time, saying *this is you*, though we might,
in fact, be many—codger at dawn, wistful child
at noon, schoolmarm at dusk, libertine
at midnight. Which is why we sometimes
envy the freedom of the man with his cart
full of rags. He's singing "Your Cheating Heart"
though he cannot sing. He's unleashing
a little dance in his duct-taped shoes.
Apropos of nothing or everything, my uncle
shouted to his sister, "I've got to make it
to The Promised Land!" "Don't we all,"
my aunt said. "Don't we all." And my stepfather,
in the throes of it, too, said, "I get bored.
Sometimes I need to do something to break up
the monopoly." But listen, at a party once,
under the influence of a very green brownie,
I'd slipped into a back room, grabbed
a black umbrella, donned a triple extra-large
safety-orange down jacket and a pair
of antique motorcycle goggles. I suddenly
understood I intended to burst into the party
and dance a ridiculous dance I had not
yet even imagined. I stood a moment
ready to enter that room filled with people,
a few of whom I knew well, many others
I had just met, and thought, *Am I*
the sort of person who would do something like this?
Before I could answer, I was dancing,
a burst and swirl, a bluster of orange and black.

THE OWL ON RATTLESNAKE DRIVE

after Richard Hugo

Great gray the breeze blew south now whirls
his head and pins you with his ochre eyes.
Cottonwoods rattle a warning. Winds no one
predicted whisper words nobody hears.

Melancholia has laid the city low. Off shift,
the nurses sip pop and chatter outside Oles.
The old man in 206 is gone, the woman
in 216 is slipping fast. Sun's first light

coronates Mount Jumbo, flirts, glittering,
in the Clark Fork's riffles, rises full, a cold coin
on the pale blue of sky. The Wylie writers
puzzle their first words, half dreamed,

half gifted by consonants cluttering the margins.
The day brings deer in the flower bed, magpies
hunkering, skittish, on the dead dog's dish.
A diagnosis, care plan, some small hope

in the wisteria's resistance—a handful of leaves
unwithered. The inversion days still months away,
the Frenchtown mill's plumes rise and dissipate
like morning dreams of fishing Rock Creek riffles.

Quick hit that breaks the rolling sheen. The call
goes up: *Fish on!* Then backpedal, backpedal.
Vain hope of keeping him upstream. The swift
downstream run instead, the dead weight

of him, until he leaps, rainbow arc and twist,
and the line goes slack. A dream. Your dream.
And yet the fish escapes. *Dream better,* your buddy
says, grinning, knee-deep in your dream's water.

So you dream a second rise, but the trashmen's
roar and clatter spooks him. Across town, the brick
buildings of the college burn a brighter red,
the grizzly yawns bronze in the grief of it.

The day shift nurses already flicking lights
and taking vitals. The children lining up
to board the purring bus. The world goes on,
tilted, spinning. The great gray shifts and dozes.

ACKNOWLEDGMENTS

"A Few Questions for M.," *Glacier*
"After the Death of Poetry," *Tampa Review*
"After Therapy, I Reimagine Our Life Together as a Series of Movie Scenes," *Plume*
"Against Deliverance," *Missouri Review*
"A Note on the Poetry," *Glacier*
"An Open Letter from My Poems," *Swing*
"Flamenco Recital," *Taos Journal of Poetry*
"In Gioiella," *Taos Journal of Poetry*
"Intention," *Santa Fe Literary Review*
"Jess," *Bennington Review*
"Legacy," *Ink in Thirds*
"Letter to Hugo from Santa Fe," *Porcupine Literary*
"The Gathering," *Raleigh Review*
"The Kettlefish," *The Wallace Stevens Journal*
"Vow," *Pine Hills Review*
"Wallace Stevens at the Craft Fair," *The Wallace Stevens Journal*
"Wallace Stevens on the Moon," *I-70*

"Wallace Stevens in the Blackfoot River Valley" appeared in *The Last Milkweed* (Tupelo Press, North Adams, MA, 2024).

"The Famous Poet," "Asterisk as Ornament," "Abjection," "The Structure of Our Grief," and "Carnal in the Land of Blood and Beauty" appeared in the chapbook *Choose Your Own America* (Finishing Line Press, Georgetown, KY, 2022).

JON DAVIS is the author of six chapbooks and seven previous full-length poetry collections, including, most recently, *Above the Bejeweled City* (Grid Books, 2021) and *Choose Your Own America* (Finishing Line, 2022). Davis also co-translated Iraqi poet Naseer Hassan's *Dayplaces* (Tebot Bach, 2017). He has received a Lannan Literary Award, the Lavan Prize from the Academy of American Poets, a Fine Arts Work Center in Provincetown Fellowship, and two National Endowment for the Arts Fellowships. His poems have appeared in numerous anthologies, including *A House Called Tomorrow: Fifty Years of Poetry; Four Quartets: Poetry in the Pandemic; Poetry is Bread; Photographers, Writers, and the American Scene; Poet's Choice; Sixty Years of American Poetry; The Best of the Prose Poem; No Boundaries: Prose Poems by 24 American Poets;* and *Telling Stories: A Writer's Anthology*. He taught creative writing and literature for thirty years, two at Salisbury University and twenty-eight at the Institute of American Indian Arts. In 2013, he founded the Low Residency MFA in Creative Writing at IAIA, which he directed until his retirement in 2018. From 2012–2014, he served as the City of Santa Fe's fourth poet laureate. He maintains a website at jondavispoet.com.

In January of 2024, Davis and poet/guitarist Greg Glazner formed the band Clap the Houses Dark. Their first album, *Clap the Houses Dark*, which mixes poetic language with complex rock compositions, is streaming on all the major platforms.